S0-BNK-120

Dodgeville Public Library
139 Iowa St.
Dodgeville, WI 53533

WITHDRAWN

Dinosaurs

Dougal Dixon

KINGFISHER

NEW YORK

Dodgeville Public Library
139 S. Iowa St.
Dodgeville, WI 53533

KINGFISHER
LONDON & NEW YORK

Copyright © Kingfisher 2010
Published in the United States by Kingfisher,
175 Fifth Avenue, New York, NY 10010
Kingfisher is an imprint of Macmillan Children's Books, London.
All rights reserved.

Illustrations by Peter Bull Art Studio
Additional illustrations by Steve and Sam Weston;
Russell Gooday and Jon Hughes/Pixel Shack

Distributed in the U.S. by Macmillan, 175 Fifth Avenue,
New York, NY 10010
Distributed in Canada by H.B. Fenn and Company Ltd.,
34 Nixon Road, Bolton, Ontario L7E 1W2

Library of Congress Cataloging-in-Publication data
has been applied for.

ISBN: 978-0-7534-6402-1

Kingfisher books are available for special promotions and
premiums. For details contact: Special Markets Department,
Macmillan, 175 Fifth Avenue, New York, NY 10010.

For more information, please visit
www.kingfisherpublications.com

Printed in China
1 3 5 7 9 8 6 4 2
1TR/0310/UNT/WKT/157MA/C

Picture credits

**The Publisher would like to thank the following
for permission to reproduce their material
(t = top, b = bottom, c = center, l = left, r = right):**
Page 4br Corbis/Louie Psihoyos; 5cl Shutterstock/Paolo
Toscani; 5bl Shutterstock/JuNe74; 8cl Shutterstock/Wesley
Pohl; 9tl Shutterstock/Anton Foltin; 9bl taburinsdino; 11br
Shutterstock/wupeng; 12cl Corbis/DK Limited; 12b Natural
History Museum, London; 13cl Natural History Museum,
London; 13ctr Shutterstock/Palis Michalis; 13cbr Natural
History Museum, London; 13br Corbis/Sandy Felsenthal;
15tr Corbis/Louie Psihoyos; 16bl Mervyn Rees/Alamy;
17c Natural History Museum, London; 19br Getty
Images/National Geographic; 21t Getty Images/Dorling
Kindersley; 23tr Nature Picture Library/Jose Luis Gomez
de Francisco; 24 Natural History Museum, London;
25tl Corbis/Louie Psihoyos; 25tr Corbis/Louie Psihoyos;
25cl Natural History Museum, London; 29t Corbis/HBSS;
29bl Corbis/Bernardo Gonzales Riga; 29br Corbis/Louie
Psihoyos; 30cr Shutterstock/Juriah Mosin; 30br
Shutterstock/Anton Foltin; 31 Shutterstock/slowfish

Contents

Choose your own journey

On some of the pages in this book, you will find colored buttons with symbols on them. There are four types of different-colored buttons, and each belongs to a journey you can follow through the book. Choose a journey, follow it through the book, and you'll find you make some interesting discoveries of your own.

For example, on page 7, you'll find a red button next to a pack of hunting dinosaurs, like this:

Page 22

Food and feeding

There is a page number in the button. Turn to that page (22) to find something else about food and feeding. Follow all of the steps through the book, and at the end of your journey, you'll find out how the steps are linked and will discover even more information about this topic.

Science

Dinosaur lives

Nature

The other journeys in this book are science, dinosaur lives, and nature. Follow a journey and see what you can discover!

What were dinosaurs?

Dinosaurs were a group of reptiles that lived between 230 and 65 million years ago (mya). They were the most important land animals during the Triassic, Jurassic, and Cretaceous periods of Earth's history.

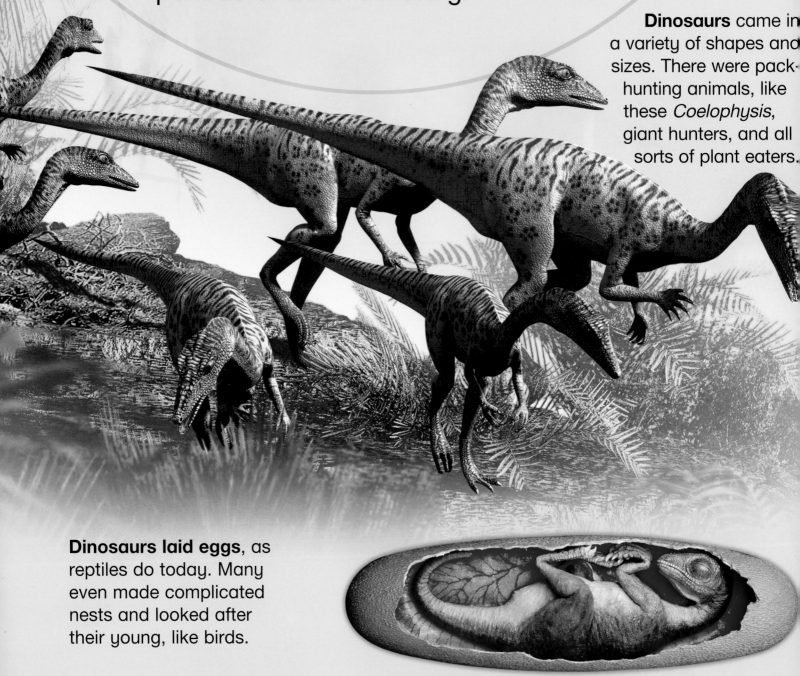

Dinosaurs came in a variety of shapes and sizes. There were pack-hunting animals, like these *Coelophysis*, giant hunters, and all sorts of plant eaters.

Dinosaurs laid eggs, as reptiles do today. Many even made complicated nests and looked after their young, like birds.

Triceratops lived at the end of the Cretaceous period.

The Cretaceous period (120 million years ago to 65 mya) saw the last of the dinosaurs. All kinds of armored and horned dinosaurs appeared.

Jurassic times (180 mya to 120 mya) were the dinosaurs' heyday. Large meat eaters evolved, and the long-necked plant eaters became the biggest land animals ever.

Diplodocus was a Jurassic plant eater.

Many dinosaurs had scaly skin.

These leathery, dinosaur-like scales belong to a modern crocodile.

By the end of the **Triassic period** (208 mya), there were all kinds of dinosaur groups, including the first big plant eaters.

Plateosaurus was an early plant eater.

Today's reptiles, like this gecko, have **legs** that stick out to the side. Dinosaurs held their legs beneath their heavy bodies.

The earliest dinosaurs appeared in the late Triassic period around 230 mya. They were swift two-footed hunters.

Eoraptor was one of the first dinosaurs.

What is this?

1 *Diplodocus*, a big plant eater

2 *Allosaurus* uses its claws to kill and tear meat.

3 *Allosaurus*, the bigge[st] Jurassic meat eater

Page 15

Meat eaters

Today, meat-eating animals eat plant-eating animals. It was exactly the same in dinosaur times. In the Jurassic period, about 150 million years ago, fierce meat-eating dinosaurs were hunting all over the world.

Page 22

A pack of hungry *Ceratosaurus* settles down to eat its kill—a baby *Diplodocus*. But then a giant *Allosaurus* leaps in to chase them away and steal the meal. While the fight rages, a swift little *Ornitholestes* darts in and snatches away a tasty piece of meat.

This is the big killing claw of an *Allosaurus*.

Fierce killers

If you look at a dinosaur skeleton, you can usually tell right away if it was a meat eater. Look for long jaws with sharp teeth and clawed hands. You'll see strong back legs for running and a small body balanced by a heavy tail.

Back is held level so that the teeth and claws are far forward.

Hands and claws are held inward for seizing prey.

The teeth at the side of *Albertosaurus* jaws (above top) were flat blades, like steak knives, for cutting meat. Those at the front (above) were thicker, for holding on to struggling prey.

Meat-eating dinosaurs are called theropods.

Giganotosaurus was one of the largest of all meat eaters. More than 40 feet (12 meters) long, it could attack and kill the biggest plant-eating dinosaurs in Late Cretaceous South America.

Allosaurus

Meat eaters had three-clawed toes.

stiff, heavy tail for balance

Allosaurus was the biggest of the Jurassic meat eaters. It stalked the plains of North America, attacking giant plant eaters or stealing the prey killed by smaller hunters.

Strong hind legs carried all of the dinosaur's weight.

Meat-eater skulls had flexible jaws that could open wide and swallow huge chunks of meat. Some were heavy and worked like hammers, bringing the upper teeth crashing down with killing force.

Ceratosaurus skull

Allosaurus used both its teeth and its claws for killing.

Jurassic giants

The heaviest, longest, and tallest animals ever to have lived on land were the sauropods. These plant-eating giants spent most of their days eating, munching through enormous amounts of food. They had long necks and tiny heads.

Page 23

Page 27

1. *Diplodocus*, a very long sauropod

2. *Diplodocus* eating leaves with its rakelike teeth

3. monkey-puzzle tree, a typical Jurassic tree

? This is a close-up of a young cycad leaf, a favorite food for sauropods.

The plains of Jurassic North America are dry places. Trees grow only along riverbanks and around lakes. The ground is covered by low-growing ferns and cycads. Big sauropods roam the landscape, eating this vegetation. Pairs of tall *Brachiosaurus* browse the high branches, like giraffes. Other sauropods feed on the middle branches or close to the ground.

Page 22

What is this?

4 *Camarasaurus*, the most common Jurassic sauropod

5 *Brachiosaurus*, one of the tallest sauropods

6 *Brachiosaurus* eating high branches

Plant-eating machines

The long-necked sauropods, the biggest land animals that ever lived, were all plant eaters and ate huge amounts of food. We can tell a lot about these dinosaurs from fossils of their long necks, stomach insides, and teeth.

Some sauropods had spines down their backs and clubs on their tails. ••••

A scientist builds a model of a sauropod skeleton.

A *Diplodocus* skeleton shows its tail raised off the ground and its neck held low. When it was alive, both were pulled up by strong tendons along the backbone.

Diplodocus was the longest known sauropod.

A sauropod had an elephant-like body, four massive legs, a tiny head on the end of a long neck, and a long tail.

Shunosaurus

So much food passed through such a tiny mouth that the sauropod had no time to chew.

conifer needles

Huge amounts of **leaves and conifer needles** made up a sauropod's diet.

Sauropods swallowed **stomach stones**, which stayed in their stomachs and helped grind up tough plant food.

A sauropod's teeth were peglike or spoon shaped, good for raking leaves and twigs from branches, not for chewing.

Brachiosaurus had a tall neck, like a giraffe. Its long vertebrae (neck bones) lifted its tiny head up to the highest trees, where its spoon-shaped teeth could scrape off leaves and twigs.

A group of *Parasaurolophus* look up suddenly. Their leader is making a loud trumpeting noise. It may mean danger, or he may be steering them away from other duckbills nearby.

Crested dinosaurs

In the late Cretaceous period, from about 100 million years ago to 65 million years ago, plant-eating dinosaurs called duckbills, or hadrosaurs, were a common sight. Many had strangely shaped crests on top of their heads.

4 *Parasaurolophus* baby with a small crest

5 *Parasaurolophus* male bellowing

6 female with curled head crest

What is this?

3

6

5

Page 30

4

Page 23

Page 26

This is a jaw full of new teeth ready to grow to replace those that get worn down.

Calls and colors

In today's world, a lion roars, a rooster crows, and a peacock shakes its tail—all are ways that these animals communicate with one another. It was the same with dinosaurs. The duckbills could communicate both by sound and by visual signals.

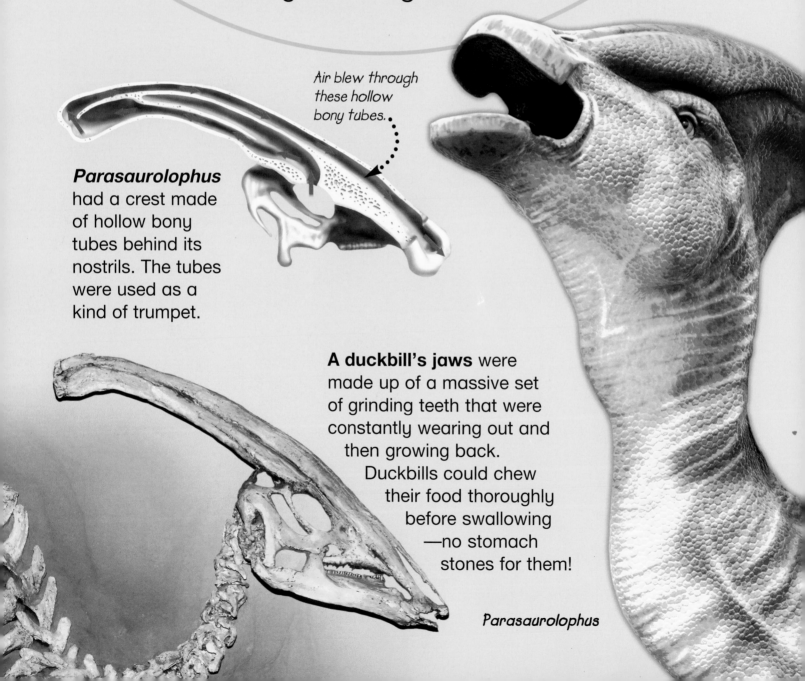

Air blew through these hollow bony tubes.

Parasaurolophus had a crest made of hollow bony tubes behind its nostrils. The tubes were used as a kind of trumpet.

A duckbill's jaws were made up of a massive set of grinding teeth that were constantly wearing out and then growing back. Duckbills could chew their food thoroughly before swallowing —no stomach stones for them!

Parasaurolophus

Anatotitan could have been this color . . .

Dinosaur colors were probably fairly bright, but we don't really know for sure. Duckbills may have had striking patterns so that they could identify one another, or they may have been camouflaged.

. . . or this color.

The sound made by a Parasaurolophus was probably like a trumpet or trombone.

Sometimes we find fossilized duckbill skin.

Although we know the skin texture, we can only guess the color.

Tsintaosaurus had a crest that stuck straight up like a unicorn's horn.

Olorotitan had a hatchet-shaped crest.

Different duckbills had different crests. Like the horns of antelope today, the crests helped duckbills identify the animals that were like them and belonged to their own herds. In addition to the different shapes, the crests would have had a range of colors, making each species truly distinctive.

Corythosaurus had a semicircular crest like an ancient Greek helmet.

Dinosaurs with armor

With so many big, fierce meat-eating dinosaurs around, it is no wonder that some of the plant-eaters evolved armor to defend themselves. Horns, plates, neck shields, and spikes all appeared on different dinosaurs.

1. *Albertosaurus,* a fierce predator

2. *Edmontonia,* protected by back armor

3. tail weapon of bladelike spikes

❓ This is part of a *Styracosaurus* skull. The gaps in the neck shield keep it from being too heavy.

Page 15

An *Albertosaurus* is hunting. It ignores the herds of horned dinosaurs—there are too many of them. Instead, it attacks a lone *Edmontonia* and is not put off by its armor and spikes.

What is this?

4 *Einiosaurus* (left) and *Triceratops* in the distance

5 *Styracosaurus* facing danger as a group

6 *Styracosaurus* with a neck shield and horn

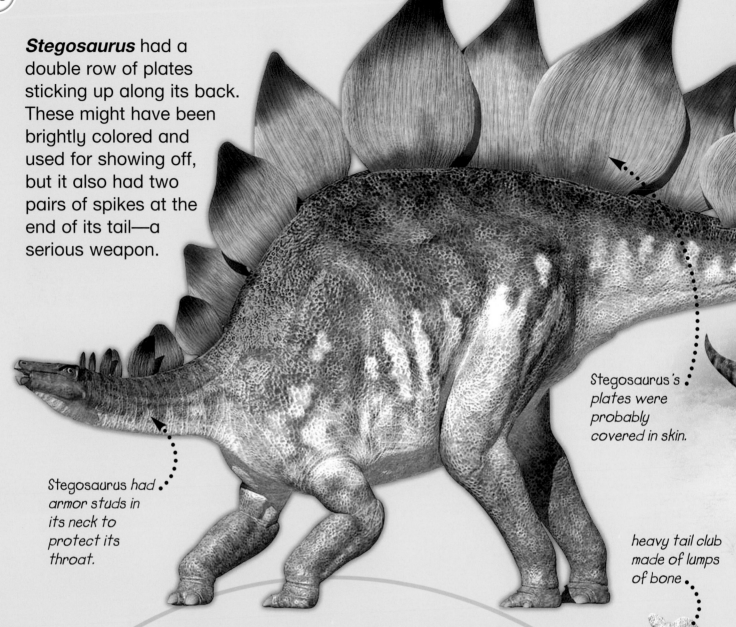

Stegosaurus had a double row of plates sticking up along its back. These might have been brightly colored and used for showing off, but it also had two pairs of spikes at the end of its tail—a serious weapon.

Stegosaurus's plates were probably covered in skin.

Stegosaurus had armor studs in its neck to protect its throat.

heavy tail club made of lumps of bone

Under attack!

Dinosaur life was an arms race! As meat eaters became bigger and fiercer, plant eaters needed more and more elaborate armor in order to defend themselves. Plant-eating dinosaurs had heavy armor made up of different combinations of plates, shields, studs, clubs, and vicious horns.

tegosaurus's tail
pikes had a core of
one and an outer
oating of horn.

Pachycephalosaurus had a bony dome on its head. This was used not only for fighting enemies—big males would have fought each other to be the leader of the herd.

bony head dome used as a battering ram

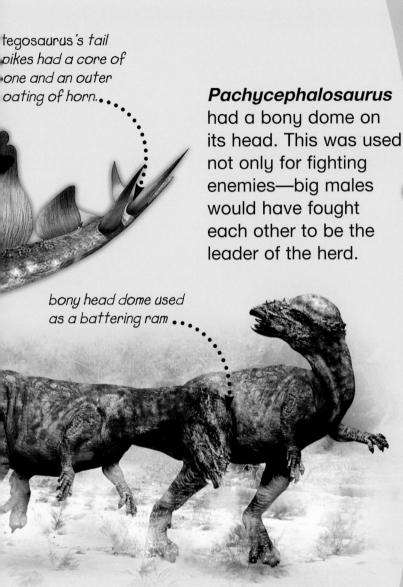

thick, bony neck shield

Triceratops was one of several dinosaurs with an armored shield around its neck. Its three horns all pointed forward. The animal would turn its armored head to face approaching danger.

An armored back and a tail club were *Ankylosaurus*'s defensive weapons. The tail was as strong and dangerous as an ax or a medieval club.

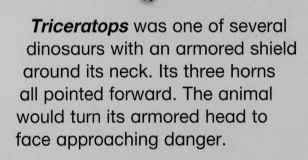

Triceratops herds may have formed a circle to protect their young.

Page 15

Page 10

Dinosaur nests

Like their descendants, the birds, dinosaurs laid eggs in nests. They had to defend their eggs and young from all kinds of attacks. Many dinosaurs nested in large groups and, when the young grew big enough, moved around in herds for protection.

What is this?

Page 27

4

5

Page 19

Troodon, a small meat eater, sits on its nest. It is part of a large colony, or group, all nesting together beside a lake during the Cretaceous period. Bigger dinosaurs, like the duckbill *Maiasaura*, nest in a colony nearby. The dinosaur parents have to guard constantly against egg stealers such as Chirostenotes.

6

¿ *Troodon* had feathers very similar to these. Which belong to a modern-day eagle.

Growing up

We know a lot about dinosaur life. Some dinosaurs lived alone, while others lived in family groups and herds. Fossil eggs and nests tell us about their early lives, and footprints show where they traveled. Sometimes fossils of entire herds are found.

Dinosaur eggs had hard shells, like those of today's birds.

Hatching was a risky time for dinosaurs. Some, like these baby *Maiasaura*, were looked after by their parents. Other dinosaurs could live on their own right away.

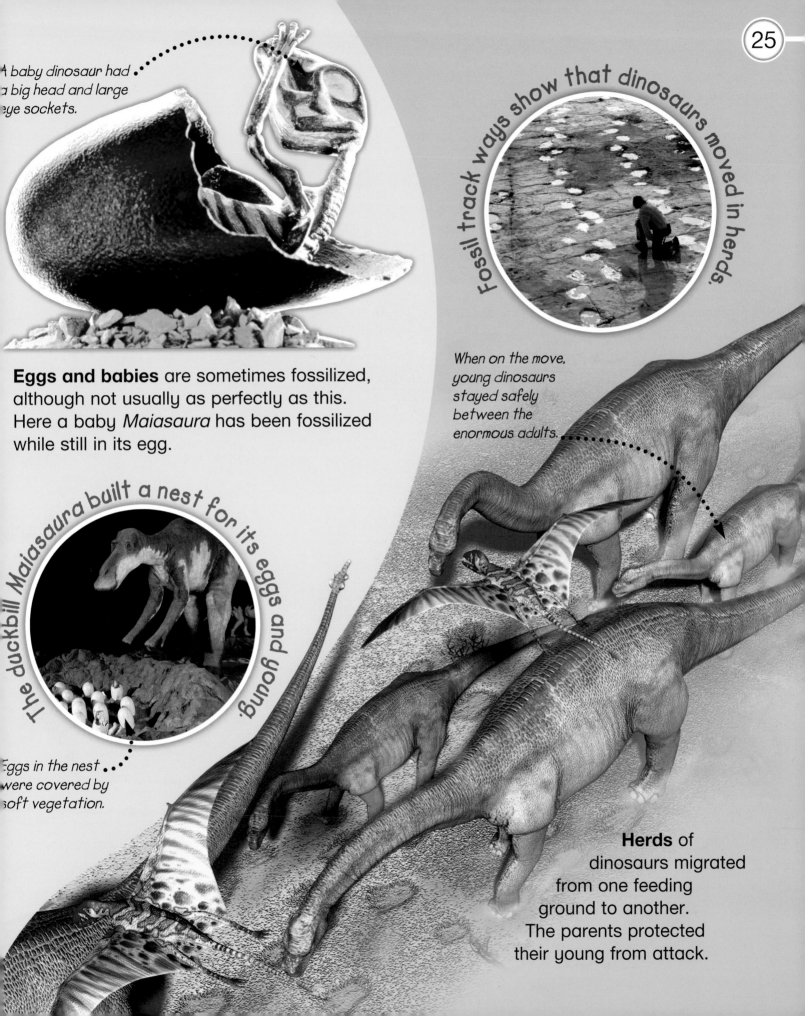

A baby dinosaur had a big head and large eye sockets.

Fossil track ways show that dinosaurs moved in herds.

Eggs and babies are sometimes fossilized, although not usually as perfectly as this. Here a baby *Maiasaura* has been fossilized while still in its egg.

When on the move, young dinosaurs stayed safely between the enormous adults.

The duckbill *Maiasaura* built a nest for its eggs and young.

Eggs in the nest were covered by soft vegetation.

Herds of dinosaurs migrated from one feeding ground to another. The parents protected their young from attack.

What is this?

1 Volcanic gases add to the damage.

2 *Triceratops*, a plant eater, faces starvation.

3 *Quetzalcoatlus*, a flyir reptile, will die out.

Page 30

What happened?

Suddenly, 65 million years ago, all of the dinosaurs vanished. We think that a giant meteorite struck Earth and caused so much damage that the dinosaurs could not survive. About 50 to 80 percent of all animal and plant life died out at this time.

3

Page 30

4

5

A meteorite hurtles through the atmosphere. A few seconds later, it will hit Earth and explode, killing everything nearby. Dust and steam thrown up will change the climate for many years. This will kill the plants and cause the death of plant-eating animals and then of meat eaters.

Page 30

6

This is a duckbill's beak. It is made of horn with a sharp edge, used for scraping twigs and leaves.

The story so far

Sometimes a dead dinosaur would fall into a river and be buried by sand. Over time, the sand would turn to rock, and the bones to mineral. Millions of years later, that rock might be worn away by the weather, revealing the fossil. Only then can we find it.

Some flowering plants survived when the dinosaurs died out.

Around 65 million years ago, the dinosaurs became extinct (died out), along with three-fourths of all other animal species. Afterward, a new set of animals evolved and repopulated Earth.

the meteorite impact

Paleontologists are scientists who study the ancient life of Earth. Through their work we can find out about the animals and plants of long ago— including the dinosaurs.

paleontologists uncovering a sauropod skeleton

Finding a whole dinosaur skeleton is rare. More often the remains are incomplete, and some dinosaurs are known from only a single bone.

Discovering dinosaurs at a museum is a lot of fun. But a mounted skeleton is the result of years of careful excavation and study.

A dinosaur at a museum is usually made from the parts of different skeletons.

Dinosaur fossils are not made of the original bone—that has been replaced by mineral.

These boxes contain fossilized dinosaur dung.

Dinosaur remains are taken to a laboratory to be studied. Different paleontologists are experts in different types of fossils. Some study bones, while others study footprints or even dung.

Ceratosaurus on the attack

Food and feeding

Some **meat eaters** hunted alone. Others hunted in packs. Small and medium-size hunters, such as *Ceratosaurus*, would have found it easier to hunt big prey in groups.

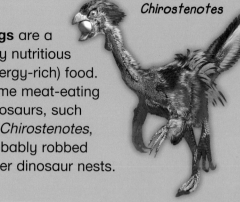

Chirostenotes

Eggs are a very nutritious (energy-rich) food. Some meat-eating dinosaurs, such as *Chirostenotes*, probably robbed other dinosaur nests.

Nature

At the start of the age of dinosaurs, Earth's **plants** were mostly ferns and conifers. There was no grass. By the end of the dinosaur age, broad-leaved trees had evolved.

Dragonfly

Insects were some of the first land creatures. They evolved 200 million years before the dinosaurs appeared. Today there are several million species of insects.

Dinosaur lives

Many dinosaurs **lived in herds** for protection against meat eaters. They migrated from one feeding ground to another as the seasons changed.

We know that at least some dinosaurs built **nests**, laid eggs, and looked after their young when they hatched—just like birds do today.

a duckbill's nest

Science

long-necked *Brachiosaurus*

If scientists find a complete dinosaur **skeleton**, they can see right away what the animal looked like. More often they find only part of a skeleton, or bones scattered around.

Fossilized footprints give us clues about dinosaur life— whether they ran or walked and how many of them moved around together. It is impossible to tell which dinosaur made which footprint, though

More to explore

Diplodocus, a sauropod

Sauropods ate plants. They were a little like vacuum cleaners, standing in one place while their long necks hosed around for food.

Tyrannosaurus, one of the biggest and last of the meat eaters, had jaw muscles that were powerful enough to crush all your bones and a mouth big enough to swallow you whole.

There were many other types of **reptiles** living during the age of dinosaurs. Crocodiles, turtles, and the ancestors of all modern lizards, like this one, scuttled around the dinosaurs' feet.

Mammals appeared when the dinosaurs did. Throughout dinosaur times, they were small and insignificant. Only when the dinosaurs died out did they become the most important animals on Earth.

Cimolestes

Some dinosaurs had clever ways of **defending** themselves from predators. *Styracosaurus* probably crowded together so that their horns and shields could protect the whole herd.

Styracosaurus

Dinosaurs could hear well, and they could also see well. Some, like the duckbills, could **communicate** with one another using visual displays and loud noises.

Parasaurolophus

Sometimes we find fossils of **dinosaur skin**. Then we can see if the animal's surface was scaly, leathery, or even feathered.

meteorite

Scientists study the **extinction** of the dinosaurs by looking at the rocks of that time—rocks full of meteorite dust, damage from tsunamis, and layers of charcoal from forest fires.

Index

WITHDRAWN